Jane Seskin's husband died of cancer.
She is the author of *Living Single, Young Widow, Getting My Head Straight,* and *Breaking Up;* is a contributor to numerous national magazines and newspapers; and lectures extensively.

A Time to Love

JANE SESKIN

A SPECTRUM BOOK

PRENTICE-HALL, INC.
Englewood Cliffs, New Jersey 07632

Library of Congress Cataloging in Publication Data

SESKIN, JANE.
A time to love.

(A Spectrum Book)
1. Widows—Poetry I. Title.
PS3569.E75T5 811'.5'4 77-2927
ISBN 0-13-921627-8

A Time to Love,
Jane Seskin

Englewood Cliffs, New Jersey 07632

A SPECTRUM BOOK

10 9 8 7 6 5 4 3 2 1

Printed in the United States of America

PRENTICE-HALL INTERNATIONAL, INC., *London*
PRENTICE-HALL OF AUSTRALIA PTY., LTD., *Sydney*
PRENTICE-HALL OF CANADA, LTD., *Toronto*
PRENTICE-HALL OF INDIA PRIVATE, LIMITED, *New Delhi*
PRENTICE-HALL OF JAPAN, INC., *Tokyo*
WHITEHALL BOOKS LIMITED, *Wellington, New Zealand*

To S.,
Who gave encouragement,
Friendship,
And Love

THANKS ARE DUE:

To my parents—

Who are always there for "Their Daughter, the Writer,"
Through the good times and the bad ones

To Stuart—

My brother and friend

To the Greenberg family: Pat, Harry,
Ronnie, Steven—

Who demonstrate love and courageous strength
To everyone they touch

To loyal, loving friends—

Ellen Schmalholz, Carolyn Goudsmit,
Susan Shapiro, Janet Harris, and Bette Ziegler

To Marcia Pollak—

Who did more than listen

To my agent, Meredith Bernstein—

Who brought the dream to reality

And finally, To Janie—

Who is alive and well
And running free!

You color
My world
With love.
The only tears
I shed
Are from laughter.
With you
I can fly
Over the rainbow.

I | YOU COLOR MY WORLD WITH LOVE

Today.
We interrupt this life
To bring you
A catastrophe.

Cancer.
A six-letter word
That sealed our fate.
Nothing
Is forever.

They told us together,
In the room that was to be your prison,
My nails biting into your flesh.
No tears that moment or that day—
We were too stunned
To comprehend, to react.
They said: "Acute Leukemia,"
As I looked out the window
Where the sun
Had the nerve to shine.
There was no clap of thunder,
No darkening of sky;
And somehow
That seemed unfair.

I ran coatless down the street,
With hair flying in the wind
That savagely froze my tears mid-cheek,
Gasping, choking for breath.
Hands outstretched,
I grasped for some bit of sanity
That could make sense
Out of this nightmare world
Into which we had been
So rudely plunged.

I guess
The joke
Is really on me.
For I grew up
Believing in the tooth fairy
And other myths of life.
So,
I just took it for granted
That you came
With
A lifetime
Guarantee.

My Aunt told me:
"God only takes the best."
I'd like to accept that blindly,
But I no longer trust my religion
And my faith is no comfort.
If
I could lean on my religion,
I might not feel
So cheated.
To me, there is no rationale
Behind a God
Who destroys
The "best."

The Cancer Ward
Was ten rooms
On the top floor of the hospital,
With their occupants waiting
For certain death.
No time limits placed on visiting,
As a token goodie
Thrown out to potential mourners.
Special nurses,
Who volunteered for this floor,
Left us alone
To make love in a crank-style bed.
We got away with murder
In our private refuge,
While they averted their faces
Out of sympathy,
Compassion,
Or pity.

A windowless room for visitors
To cry in.
I sat alone,
Huddled up in a plastic-covered chair.
Artificial flowers surrounded me—
Another denial of life,
Covered with dust,
Waiting for attention that did not come.
I clutched a box of tissues
Stamped: "Compliments of the Hospital"
And waited
And wondered,
"Why Us?"

In a spotless office
With checked linoleum
Covering the floor,
The two of us
Faced each other
Across a grey metal desk.

She was a woman
God knows how old,
Unmarried,
Grey-haired,
Social worker.
Eyes never wavered
Behind rimless glasses
As she asked me
(As if inquiring about the weather):
"Do you have
A burial plot?"

I'm tired
Of being nice to you.
I feel
Like I'm walking a balance beam
And tottering.
I'm afraid to say something
That might hurt you,
While I store up resentment
Against you.
At the hospital today,
Instead of my usual cheery hello,
I walked in—
And walked back out.
You were chained to your room
Because of isolation procedures,
So that I was safe to cry,
Echoingly alone,
Out in the sterile, white hall.

Let my health and strength
Ooze into your body.
I hope
That it's my blood,
Donated
Just yesterday,
Now filtering
Into your veins.

It was supposed to be
In sickness and in health . . .
I want to be one with you.
I'd like to share
Some of your suffering,
To experience the pain
And the agonizing discomfort
That you're living through.

I want to be one with you.
I'd like to cut my hand
'Til the blood flows freely,
Or break my ankle
So I'd need a cast,
Or fall down a flight of stairs—
The bruises
A constant reminder of the hurt.

(continued)

I want to be one with you.
Let me have
My portion of pain.

I repeatedly ask myself
How to fill a year with love?
How do you say everything
That is in your heart?
How do you cram into a shortened lifetime
Unfilled years of emotion and feeling?

Through walking and talking,
By sharing and caring,
Through holding and unfolding.

I'm frightened of the future,
Scared of being alone.
How will I cope
Or manage my life
As a single person?
I have become dependent on *him*,
A reflection of his mood and mannerisms,
So used to being a part of someone else
That I doubt me
And my capacity to function
As a separate,
Unique individual.
Achingly, I realize too late
That I don't know how to behave
By myself
And that I'm terribly, horrifyingly afraid
Of growing up,
And old,
Without him.

Pain killers,
Steroids,
Anti-depressants.
So God-damn many drugs
With names I couldn't pronounce
Distorted your fine-lined body.

Puffy cheeks once so smooth,
Swollen belly once so firm,
Loss of hair from curly head.
I turned away when you touched me,
My young hero with the football physique
No longer handsome, virile, or strong.

When I faced myself,
I hurt like Hell
From shame.
For how could I
Ever say to you:
"Darling, you repulse me."

Big-named specialists
Came for consultations.
They talked in a group outside his room
In hushed voices—
Ignoring me for I was just "the wife"
And too dumb to understand.
There came a time though
When those men in white
Could no longer avoid me.
So, with heads down,
Studying the floor,
They said, in tones reserved for funerals:
"Don't worry. Have hope."

Since time had softened the blow,
And I had accepted the prognosis,

Whose mind were they really setting at ease,
Mine
Or theirs?

I am ready to bargain for his life.
Let him live
And I will devote my life to nursing.
Let him live
And I will donate my blood
As often as they let me.
Let him live
And you can have me instead.

My God, or specialists,
Or anyone who will listen:
I will do anything,
Anything—
If you will just
Let him live.

I've shared the visitor's room
With Mrs. T
For the past six mornings.
Her husband is dying
Of lung cancer.
Yes, I'm sorry for them—
But not overly sad.
Hell, he's seventy-two years old,
Married forty-four years,
Eleven grandchildren.
They've had a good, long, happy life
Together,
While we
Haven't even started.

A remission
(joy, joy, joy!)
Has set you free
To return to the world of the living.
Our lives pick up
Where we left off;
We go about our respective jobs,
And we love
A lot.
I stay awake nights
Watching you sleep,
Listening to your labored breathing.
Thinking
That this all must be
Some colossal trick
And when you wake tomorrow
You will be
Miraculously
Cured!

How lucky
For me
That you're not
A coward.

Head on—
Facing each other
Across the dining room table—
We talk,
Communicate,
And share
Our new-found feelings
On death.

Our friends won't talk about death.
They submerge your dying
Under plans for next year and the future
And the good things to come.
I want to shake them
Into understanding
That there's not much time left.
But it's no use.
If it could be you,
Then it could be them,
And that thought—
That we are all mortal—
Is too harsh, too frightening a concept
For our friends
To confront.

Dinner out
Of Chinese food,
Great until dessert.
A simple fortune cookie
Tells the tale.
He unfolds his cryptic message,
"Long life to you,"
And
Laughs.

My mind whispers:
He is dying,
He is dying,
He is dying.

So today
I will do a laundry,
Vacuum the carpet,
Defrost the refrigerator,
Clean the bathtub,
Wash the floors,
And try my very best
To forget
What *is*.

I did something tonight
That I've never done before.

My hand hurts
From slapping you
Across the mouth.
And I hurt
Way deep inside of me
From anger, deprivation, and longing.
You said to me
In a calm and quiet voice:
"Jane. No baby.
You're young, bright, and attractive.
You'll have an easier time
Remarrying
If you're a single woman."

(continued)

I slapped you then,
Hard,
And ran from the room,
Slamming the door
On my tears.

I hate women
Impregnated with love.
Their bloated bellies mock me
In the supermarket and on the street.
I am counselled by a Doctor;
"A wise decision," he said.
Ha!
What does he know?
Can he feel my emptiness
Named "what will never be"?
No blue-eyed, curly-red-haired baby,
No Mommy to be,
And no Daddy
Ever.

I looked at you
Sitting
In our big old over-stuffed armchair,
With familiar pipe in mouth,
Head bent over a book,
And my heart
Was full.

The prognosis seemed to whirl me around,
Stand me on my ear,
And make me conscious
Of all the little things you've done
That I've taken for granted.
I must not forget
To tell you tonight
That last week you looked so handsome
I was ready to seduce you
Instead of going to the party.
Did I ever tell you
That I liked the way you laugh?
And without you
I wouldn't know how to play poker,
Or lay a fire,
Or ride a motorbike,
Or be proud of my legs,
Or even like my freckles?

(continued)

Do you know
That your love
Has made me a better person,
And that I'm terribly glad you came
into my life?
Your dying is teaching me
To touch you now,
To tell you immediately
How good you make me feel,
To react honestly
Without holding back.
You've made me
Look more closely,
Listen more carefully,
And generally expanded my world.
There's no time left
To be playing cutesy games.

(continued)

I want you to know
At the moment
How much you mean
To me.

Breathe in . . .
Breathe out . . .
Slowly now,
Count to three.

I live
For the moment,
The hour,
The period of now.
Just taking one day
At a time.

Up with the sun
To begin a trip
For a day at the beach.
Wet from the ocean,
Drying off with the sun,
Food and wine
And him sleeping soundly beside me.

Water, shockingly tingly fresh;
Sun and sand
And a blanket in a cool pungent cave.
Slowly making love
With love;
Easy, tender, searing climax,
To fall asleep
In each other's arms.

(continued)

Hand in hand
We walk to the car
Under a sky of fire and smiling faces.
Life and my love—I am gloriously happy.

Home at night,
We unpack
And shower together.
I watch you take your eighteen pills
In three swallows as illness intrudes.
Reality impinges
Upon our sunburned bodies
Touching under the covers,
And
I am sleeping
With a dead man.

The doctor gave me a pill
To calm me down,
And for a couple of hours
Today
I floated in a world
That contained no tragedy.
I escaped
Into a more promising existence,
Achieving a state of being
Where my spirit was comforted,
With hope and miracles
No longer words
But actual promises.

When I have time to think
Then I am bitter that it's you,
And not the thief,
The murderer,
Or the rapist.
Someone told me today
That: "The good die young."
But how can I accept
That rationalization
When my heart is crying tears?

I hate you today.
Don't talk to me.
Don't come too close.
Stay out of my way.
You,
You've ruined my life.
Yes, you,
The bright young man
With
"Potential."

God damn it,
Lose your temper!
Scream in frustration!
Roar in anger!
React!

Stoically you accepted the verdict,
While I walked around
Trembling,
On the verge
Of hysteria.

Sickness
Didn't elevate you
To Sainthood.
You still leave the bathroom
In a mess,
Bite your nails,
And refuse to help me
Do the dishes.
But maybe
Knowing that you're going to die
Reduces your faults
Or my basis for arguments
To trivia,
Which in reality
Is what they are.
The fact is that you're alive
Now
And that you can
Make me laugh and smile
And still appreciate life.

Your flesh
Against my flesh,
Inside of me,
As one.
We move together,
A joyous unit
In perfect rhythm and harmony.
Reaching heights
Together
Only dreamed of.

I have a job to do:
I must keep smiling.
Today I became
So absorbed in a project
That the time
Slipped away
And I found
I enjoyed myself
Without once thinking
Of death.
I must keep smiling.

But was I wrong?

How low
Can I sink?

My head is fuzzy
With cotton candy,
My arms are quivering
Like jelly,
And there's a heaviness
In my thighs
That makes me want
To melt
Into the bed—
Diving for oblivion.

You've been hospitalized
Again.

If I were hooked up to those tubes,
My body
Assaulted and humiliated
Constantly,
Day in and day out,
I think I would rather
Commit suicide.

I pause to consider,
Gratefully,
That we were together
For six good years.
Some people
Never have
As much.

You didn't die like in the movies,
With arms crossed on your chest,
Eyes closed in peaceful sleep.

No one had prepared me
For convulsive muscle spasms,
Your body jerking around without control.
They told me you were dead,
While your body continued its awkward,
  pulsating life
On its own.
Didn't it know?

Shrieking hysterically,
I held you in my arms
Until they pulled me away.
Somehow I was in the hall when darkness
  descended
And I fell to the floor,
Mercifully.

My first funeral
Was yours.
I arranged everything with you in mind.
There could be no hypocrisy
Surrounding this last right
I owed you.
Sounds funny to say:
You would have been proud to attend.
There were flowers—only mine,
The carnations you used to bring me
As unexpected treats.
I wore my only black dress,
The special one reserved for concerts
And splurging in fancy restaurants.
A hip young guy read poetry
And talked of peace and brotherhood.
Friends held hands and cried.
I fainted, three times.

(continued)

Older relatives had no understanding
Of what was taking place.
The Hell with them,
For this funeral
Was for you.

Can you ever mourn
Without food?
The after-the-funeral,
Catered affair
Sticks in my throat.
The chopped liver made my eyes tear,
I couldn't swallow the nutted fruit cake
without choking,
And Manischewitz wine was sweet and heavy
going down.
Instead of
"What a fine man,"
It's
"The fish is good, yes?"
Not
"He had so much to give,"
But
"So have a piece of brisket."

(continued)

And instead of
"We will miss him,"
It's
"I'll bring delicatessen tomorrow."

They patted my shoulder
And said: "Don't worry.
It's going to be
All right."
But they can't see
The bruises across my eyes
Where I can still see
His body,
Burning with fever,
Writhing in pain,
Waiting out death.
Those well-meaning people
Have no knowledge
Of the lacerations on my heart
From missing my very best friend,
From losing the warmth of a well-known
body,
And of our mutual need
For our together kind of love.

Cancer
Is not a *Dirty word.*
What is dirty
Is everyone's reluctance
To talk about it.

One week.

My parents took me away
To the sun,
Where I sat in a lounge chair
Trying to bake out my thoughts.
Paralysis had set in,
Numbing my mind and body.
I just wanted to be
Left alone.

Two weeks.

I went from my parent's protection
To *his* custody.
I couldn't do a thing for myself.
I've never changed a light bulb,
Hung a picture,
Waxed a floor,
Or written a check.
He left me an imcompetent little girl
With no life insurance.
I'll never even be
A wealthy widow.

Three weeks.

The daily telephone calls
Have trickled away
To one, maybe two.
Dinner invitations,
That first week
Too numerous to keep track of,
Are no longer
Being issued.
People feel
That the crisis is over,
And so they return to the routines of
their lives
While I mourn
Alone.

It would be so easy
To lie here in bed,
Hazy from a drug-induced sleep,
Curled up in a fetal ball
With the covers up to my nose,

Day,

    After day,

        After day.

I sometimes feel
Locked
In a block of ice,
Too cold
To touch.

There seems to be
A very fine line
Between appearing stable
And having a nervous breakdown.
Almost any reminder
Of you
Begins to set me up
To set me off.

Which side
Shall I walk down?

Blank, empty, white space.
A sterile room
And me.
An apartment of my own
To hide out in
Until I regain some hold
Over my life
And figure out what it means
To
Be
Alone.

It wouldn't matter
If
I were shipwrecked
On a desert island.
And it wouldn't matter
If
I were sitting
In Shea Stadium
During the World Series.
It really wouldn't matter
Where I was,
Because
In either place
I'd still be
In isolation.

Sublimation.
I have been eating
Like a condemned person.
Gluttony
Feeds my resentment
At disjunction.
In self-pity and anger
I stuff my face,
Wanting and needing
The accumulated poundage,
The self-imposed
Untidy ugliness
To hide behind.

Lying in bed
Alone
On a Sunday morning.
Blinds pulled up
To watch the sky unleash its anger
Through darkness at eleven a.m.
The screaming wind
Smashes the rain against my window
With murdering fury.

You,
Under the ground,
Do you feel the rain
Beat a tattoo
On your chest?

I wonder.

Slowly
The apartment takes shape:
I buy things
That say "Jane."
Color splashes the walls
As it simultaneously infuses my life.
There is a job I like
With new people.
The hours
Are being filled.
I am surviving.

The living have no time
For my tears or tantrums,
And maybe that is all to the good,
For I am being swept along
In my work.
I am becoming involved
With other people,
And
I like it!

Paul and Donna
(You were their best man)
Are getting a divorce.
(Our weddings were two weeks apart.)
What do you think
About that?

I have an overwhelming feeling
Of sadness
That is not relieved
Through tears.
A watermelon has settled
In my stomach,
My mouth clenched shut
To hold in the pits.
I want to scream away
My aloneness.
But for now,
Right at this moment
In my life,
I can only remain
Choked up
And bloated.

I can't seem to find
A sense of peace.
Guilt rides my shoulders
Until I feel like a hunchback.
Why
Did I
Survive?

Three months.

I am fearful
That if I care for someone,
Make a commitment
To love a man
Freely and easily,
Trusting and vulnerable,
Then he will die.
Maybe
I've become
A jinx.

There are uneasy dinners
With your friends,
Where I am an outsider.
And coupled parties
Where I go alone.
No one talks about you
Or even mentions your name.
It's like you never existed.
My presence
Is a haunting, uncomfortable reminder
Of another time.
Please understand,
I need to make new friends.

Why is it
That you have to lose something
Before you realize
How special it was?

I walked
Behind a couple
Tonight
As the sun was setting.
A mystical time of day,
With spring in the air.
They,
The couple,
Arm in arm,
Looking, laughing,
Touching each other.
Happy.
I felt
Like kicking them
In the shins.

Life.
They can put a man on the moon
Yet let him die on the earth.

Seven months.

I took off my wedding band today,
Giving up the knowledge
   to the outside world
That someone wanted me enough
To marry me.
I tell myself
It's going to be okay.
I'm going to make it
As a person,
My own being,
No longer in need of a little gold band
To signify
Who I am.

Your death
Made me appreciate
The miracle of life.

My mind is waking up,
And I've been accepted
For graduate school.
I'm ready now
To accept the challenge,
Belatedly realizing
I've got a self
That's howling
For recognition.

Eight months.

I felt like a virgin last night.
He was no one for the future,
Rather
An old friend from the past.
My first time since you died,
And I realized
That it was all right
To make love.

"Love," you had said,
Holding me close,
"Will come again."
And so I wait
For a love,
Not like ours,
Because it could never be duplicated,
But for another kind
On a different plane.
And I will be ready
To try again
Only
Because of you.

I walked down the street
Carrying on a monologue
Of memories.

I remembered
Sitting under that tree,
Walking past that store,
Eating in that restaurant
With you.

We laughed 'til tears ran down our cheeks
On that bench
Over there in the park
And rode bicycles down this street
On the first day of spring.

(continued)

You told me you loved me
Under that street light—
As we stood in that doorway
Out of the rain,
Kissing and holding each other
Close.

The memories
In their vividness,
At first so tormenting and hurtful,
Have dimmed with time,
Memories
That I can now softly smile at,
Recalling them
With tenderness.

My best friend said:
"Jane,
This widow trip
Has got to stop.
You're getting to be
A drag."

I guess that's why
She's my best friend.

Nine months.

Hallelujah! I've found a man
Who loves me
Despite my faults,
Understands my doubts,
And is patient, gentle, and tender.
I've found a man
Who cares
About *me.*

My man makes me feel
Special.
I've told him
All about you,
And he is secure enough
As a person
Not to feel threatened.
He is calm and kind and reassuring.
He softly strokes away
My passing torment.
He is helping me to understand
And accept
That I don't have to lead a life
Of desperate self-reproach.

One year.
Anniversary.

I didn't visit the cemetery.
I was too physically ill,
My body burning with fever,
My mind too numbed to think,
Incoherent,
Without speech,
Wildly out of my head.

Violently sick,
The day passed
Without my recognition.

I can't remember
How you look.
I am no longer able
To conjure up your face
At will.
Time is passing,
And each day
You fade a little more
From my vision.
It frightens me
That you're becoming
A dream.

It's a delight to laugh,
A joy to be happy.
We see each other
Almost every night
At his place
Or mine.
My heart sings durıng the day
In anticipation of our evening.
Wow,
It's damn good
To be alive!

We're learning
From each other,
Exploring ideas and feelings.
We share
Our new experiences
Like kids
On Christmas morning.

Months pass.

The affair is over
And he did not die.
I said: "Enough,
I want to be free."
I've started to look at men
In stores, on the street,
Everywhere.

Dear first lover:
Thank you.
You've given me back my self,
Security as a woman,
Courage to enter the social world,
Knowledge that I can still be wanted,
Desired,
And loved.

We are all
Mourners.

The break-up of a marriage,
An affair,
A friendship
Unites
Us all
Through pain and sadness.

Every ending,
Though,
Makes way
For a new beginning.

I've shaved my legs,
Started taking the pill,
Bought a sexy black nightgown,
And scrubbed the underside
  of the toilet seat.

I guess you could say
I'm ready.

I am dating:
Short, tall,
Fat, thin,
Young, old
Men.

There seems to be
A parade of male people
In polyester pants,
Their middles defined
Through the courtesy of belts
By patent leather.

Woke up
To one God-damn beautiful,
Sunny day.
And, in contrast to the weather,
I mourn—
Not specifically for him
Or the men
Who have entered my life
For different periods of time,
But rather
I grieve
For all the memories
Of shared experiences
When I was
A part
Of a couple.

Weeks pass
When I don't think of you.
My life is filling up
And I am running,
Doing,
Going,
Meeting,
Making dates.
Time is rushing by
While I search
Frantically,
For fun.

Holidays
Where I am alone
Devastate me.

I made no plans
And was caught—
  Lonely,
  Tearful,
  Depressed.

I must prepare
For these occasions
Ahead of time,
So I can take comfort
In companionship.

Single,
Mingle,
Swingle.
Is that what
Being *alone*
Is all about?

Two years
Of afternoons
And evenings.

I've got another degree!
Returning to school
Strengthened my new feelings
Of self-reliance
And self-worth.
Hey, World, Listen!
I am more than surviving,
I am functioning!

I went to the cemetery today
And freaked out.
They played music
In the office
Where I went to get the number
Of your grave.
The card bearing your name
Popped out
Of an automated revolving file.
Found the site,
Covered with ivy.

It didn't really look
Six feet long.

Do you have enough room?

I long for the arm of a man
Around me in the movies
On a Saturday night.

I don't make it
In the singles bars.
I get dressed
In what I consider
Proper bar attire
Yet still don't fit in.
Maybe it's my face,
Or posture,
Or perhaps my attitude.
Whatever,
There's got to be
A better way
To meet men.

A week-long
Cruise.

I never met
So many people
Anxiously running
Through life
Searching
For
A meaningful relationship.

I'm afraid of being sick
While alone.
Sore throats and colds
I can understand and deal with;
Pains of unknown origin
Make me behave
Irrationally

At four this morning
I washed and dried my hair
Because I was positive
I was having an appendicitis attack
And wanted to look my best
When I entered the hospital.

I didn't know
  —Which hospital I should go to,
  —What friend to call to accompany me,
  —If my doctor made home visits,
  —Or even where to reach him.

(continued)

So I sat on my bed reading until daylight,
When the pains subsided
To the point of simple indigestion.

At nine I was on the phone
Establishing my support systems
As a single person.

Rap groups.

It's nice to know
That other people
Share
The same crazies
I sometimes feel
About
Living single.

A cocktail party.

He spent
Eight minutes with me,
Six with the redhead,
And not quite fifteen
With the brunette
In the corner.
His mouth and hands
Moved simultaneously
As he jotted down
Our numbers
In a little black book.

Later, at home
Instead of feeling
Pleased
At the prospect of a date,

(continued)

I only felt
A tremendous sense
Of weariness.

The art of communication
Seems to have been replaced
By the art of "making time."

Skiing vacation
By myself.

Didn't break a leg,
Did pick up two eligible men.
Handled everything—
Reservations, tips, etc.—
Okay.
Didn't introduce myself
As "widow";
Score one up
For me.

Childlike bursts
Of unprovoked laughter.
A shoulder to cry on.
Dinners,
Movies,
Company on Saturday nights.
Grateful
For warm, supportive
Women Friends.

We are all terminal.

The only difference
Between me
And the hospital patient
Is the irrefutable fact
That a time limit
Has been placed on his body and soul.

Blissfully ignorant
Of such dates,
I sometimes fall into the trap
Of taking things for granted.

I must remember
That I, too, am terminal.

Stop!
I've been rushing around
Seeking experiences
In the great human adventure.

Stop!
I told myself tonight.
I can no longer keep up the pace,
Nor do I want to.

Stop!
I need to wind down.
I need a quiet time
Where I can get to know me
And then relax
In that awareness.

Solitude
Is all right.
I am learning
To be alone with myself,
Comfortably.
I like,
Need,
And want
My private time.

The more I talk
About death,
The less
I fear it.

The less I fear death,
The more I accept it
As a part of life.

Accepting death
Makes my daily life
So much richer.

A special man,
An evening
With wine and romance.
Did you know
They turn down the bed
At the Plaza Hotel
And
Leave chocolates
On the night table?

Today
I signed a contract
With myself. .

I will not wait
Until I retire
To enjoy my life.
It is mine at the moment,
And I mean to live it well.

I vow to make my survival
So significant
That when my moment of death comes
I shall have
No regrets.

I wonder if you'd recognize me
And want me for your wife.
The change is more than physical.
Yes, I do look different;
I'm blond and thin.
That's the outside.
The inner me
Is on the way to winning a battle
For independence.
My spirit is being healed
And good things are possible
And happening.
I'm growing up,
And I wonder
If I'd want you
For my husband.

My handshake with death
Has reordered my priorities.
Instead of all my "should's"
And "ought to's,"
I need to concentrate
On my "want to's."

Three years, five months.

I am in love.
I walk around with a smile on my face.
He is as different from you
As day is to night,
And I love him—
My God, how I love him—
In a totally new,
Deeply satisfying,
Very special way.

Some day
I want
To remarry.

I want
A legal live-in friend
And lover.
I want to carry the weight
Of an unborn child.

I had a lick
Of the happiness cake;
I look forward
To a bite.

Sad times,
Happy times,
Good times,
Bad times.

All time is prime.

Moments of laughter,
Moments of tears,
Moments of anger,
Moments of fears.

All time is prime.

Working,
Going,
Resting,
Growing.

All time is prime.

God forbid
I should remain
Just "a widow."
I no longer need
That title
To define my role
In life.

Today
I am many people:
A daughter,
A sister,
A sexual being,
A writer,
An educator,
A joyous, single woman.

Let the world take note
That I have signed on
For the duration.